TONY
STEWART

by Matt Scheff

NASCAR
HEROES

Published by ABDO Publishing Company, PO Box 398166, Minneapolis, MN 55439. Copyright © 2013 by Abdo Consulting Group, Inc. International copyrights reserved in all countries. No part of this book may be reproduced in any form without written permission from the publisher. SportsZone™ is a trademark and logo of ABDO Publishing Company.

Printed in the United States of America,
North Mankato, Minnesota
112012
012013

Editor: Chrös McDougall
Series Designer: Becky Daum

Photo Credits: Cal Sport Media/AP Images, cover, title, 28-29, 30 (bottom); Autostock/Russell LaBounty/AP Images, cover; David Graham/AP Images, 4-5, 23; Todd Warshaw/AP Images, 6-7; Times-Republican, Fritz Polt/AP Images, 8-9; Tom Strattman/AP Images, 10, 30 (top); Amy Sancetta/AP Images, 11; Chris O'Meara/AP Images, 12-13; Craig Williby/AP Images, 14-15; Jim Topper/AP Images, 16-17; P. Kevin Morley/AP Images, 18; Jose Fernandez/AP Images, 19, 30 (center); Rusty Jarrett/Getty Images, 20-21; Terry Ranna/AP Images, 22; Carolyn Kaster/AP Images, 24-25, 31; Nigel Kinrade/AP Images, 26-27

Cataloging-in-Publication Data
Scheff, Matt.
 Tony Stewart / Matt Scheff.
   p. cm. -- (NASCAR heroes)
Includes bibliographical references and index.
ISBN 978-1-61783-667-1
1. Stewart, Tony, 1971- --Juvenile literature. 2. Stock car drivers--United States--Biography--Juvenile literature. I. Title.
796.72092--dc21
[B]

2012946315

CONTENTS

Tony Stewart, left, leads Carl Edwards at the 2011 Ford 400.

CLUTCH PERFORMANCE

It was the Ford 400, the final race of the 2011 National Association for Stock Car Auto Racing (NASCAR) Sprint Cup season. Tony Stewart was battling Carl Edwards for the series championship. But Stewart was in trouble. He had a hole in his grille. He had to come into the pits. He dropped to 40th place.

Stewart takes the checkered flag at the 2011 Ford 400 to win the Sprint Cup title.

Stewart got back on the track. He passed car after car. He took over the lead when Edwards stopped for fuel. Stewart's fuel tank was almost empty. But he had just enough. Stewart won the race. Edwards took second. They were tied in points. But Stewart won the tiebreaker because he had won more races. He was the Sprint Cup champion!

FAST FACT

Before 2011, the Cup Series had never had a season-ending tie.

YOUNG AND FAST

Anthony Wayne Stewart was born May 20, 1971, in Columbus, Indiana. He started racing go-karts at age seven. He won his first title a year later. He won the World Karting Association championship in 1987.

Tony soon became a legend racing midgets and other vehicles in the United States Auto Club (USAC). In 1995, he won the top three USAC championships. No one had ever won the "triple crown" before.

Tony Stewart's nickname is "Smoke." As a teenager, he often spun his rear tires, causing them to smoke.

Many young drivers start out in the World Karting Association.

FROM OPEN-WHEEL TO STOCK

Stewart joined the Indy Racing League (IRL) in 1996 to race open-wheel cars. A year later, he won the IRL championship. He finished third in 1998.

Stewart liked racing open-wheel cars in the IRL. But there was greater competition in stock cars. So Stewart joined NASCAR's Cup Series full-time in 1999. He drove the No. 20 Pontiac for the Joe Gibbs Racing (JGR) team.

Stewart prior to the 1996 Indianapolis 500

*Stewart leads at the
1996 Indianapolis 500.*

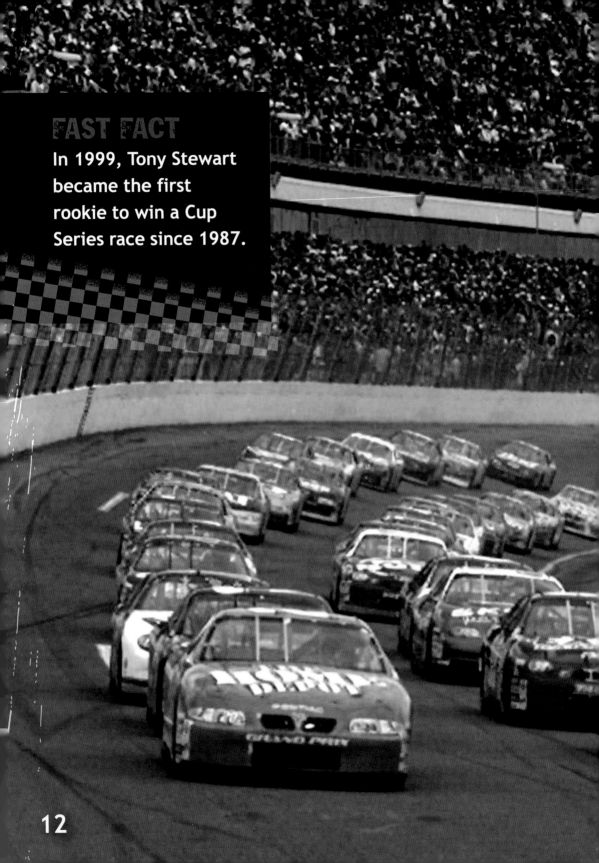

FAST FACT

In 1999, Tony Stewart became the first rookie to win a Cup Series race since 1987.

ON TO NASCAR

Racing stock cars is very different from racing open-wheel cars. Many open-wheel stars struggle when they move to NASCAR. But not Stewart. He won three races and finished fourth in the points standings. He was also the 1999 Cup Series Rookie of the Year.

Stewart, front left, *heads for Turn 1 to start the 1999 Daytona 500.*

Stewart won six Cup Series races in 2000. He was also getting a reputation. Drivers and fans thought he had a quick temper. He got into arguments with other drivers, including Jeff Gordon. Some said that Stewart drove too aggressively.

Stewart crosses the finish line first in a 2000 race at Michigan International Speedway.

Stewart's car flies through the air during a crash at the 2001 Daytona 500.

SEEKING A TITLE

Stewart's 2001 season started out rough. His car flipped over several times after a crash at the Daytona 500. Stewart came back to finish second that season. But troubles with his temper continued.

FAST FACT

Tony Stewart completed "the double" in 1999 and 2001. That meant he ran both the Indianapolis 500 in an IndyCar and a Cup Series race in a stock car in the same day.

conseco.co

FAST FACT

Tony Stewart has won titles in stock cars, IndyCars, open-wheel midgets, sprint cars, and Silver Crown cars. No other driver has won in all those categories.

Stewart crosses the finish line first at a 2002 race at Richmond International Speedway.

Stewart at Homestead-Miami Speedway in 2002

The 2002 season started poorly, too. Stewart finished in last place at the Daytona 500. But then he got hot. He won three races and had 15 top-five finishes. Stewart beat Mark Martin by 63 points to win his first Cup Series title.

IN THE CHASE

Stewart struggled for the next two seasons. He won just two races in each of them. In 2004, NASCAR added the Chase for the Cup. Stewart qualified for this playoff. But he crashed in the first race. He ended the season in sixth place.

Stewart takes a practice lap before a 2004 race at Michigan International Speedway.

Stewart's crew celebrates as he completes a victory lap at the 2005 Pepsi 400 at Daytona International Speedway.

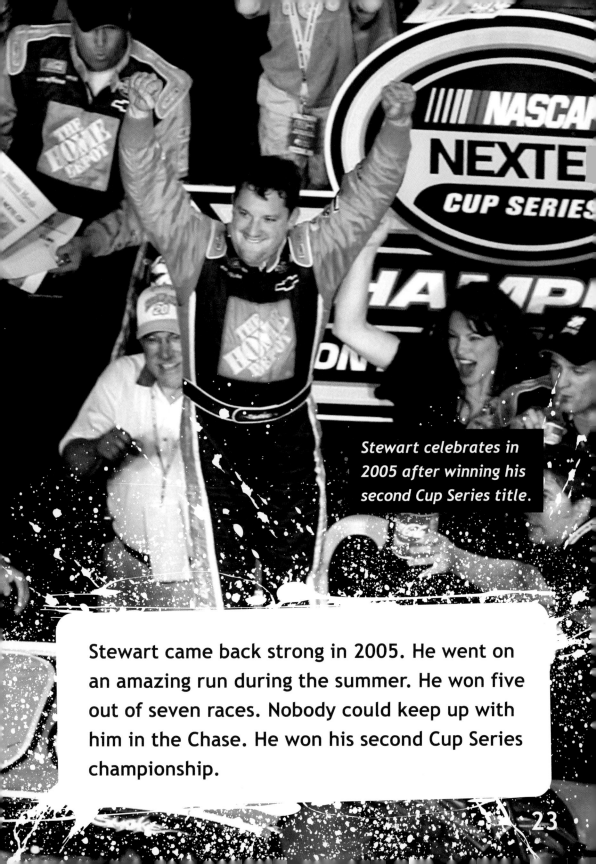

Stewart celebrates in 2005 after winning his second Cup Series title.

Stewart came back strong in 2005. He went on an amazing run during the summer. He won five out of seven races. Nobody could keep up with him in the Chase. He won his second Cup Series championship.

Stewart races at Pocono Raceway in Pennsylvania in 2008.

OWNER AND CHAMPION

Stewart's team remained near the top of the sport for the next three years. But they did not win any more titles. It was time for a change. Stewart left JGR after the 2008 season. He joined Gene Hass to form Stewart-Hass Racing.

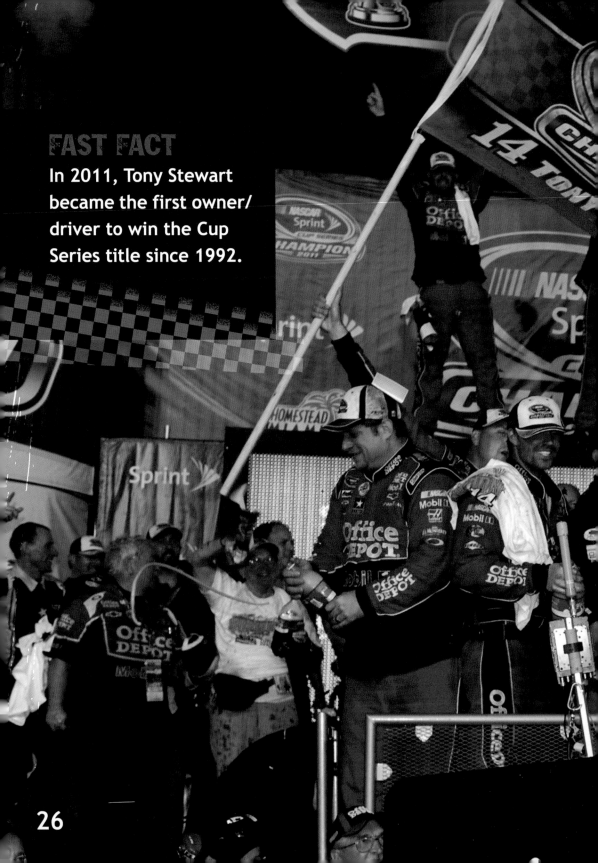

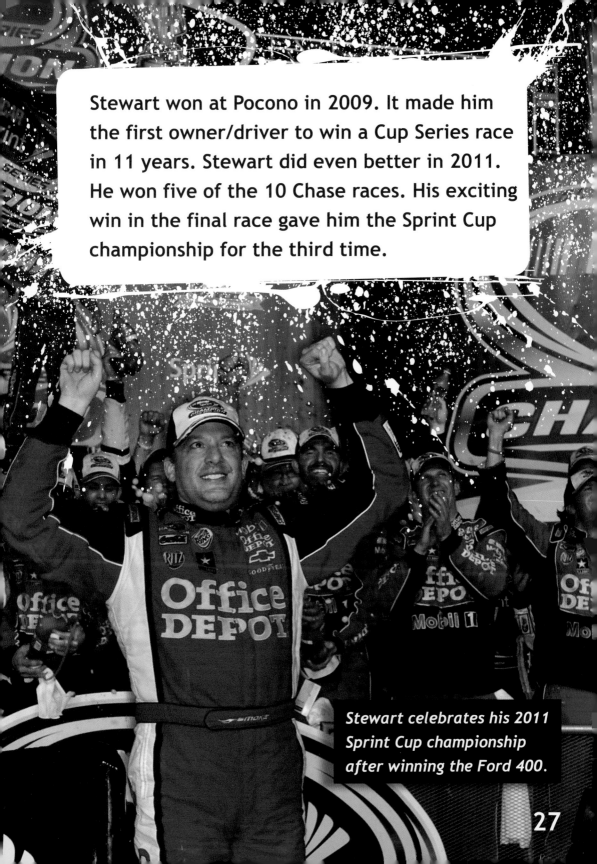

Stewart won at Pocono in 2009. It made him the first owner/driver to win a Cup Series race in 11 years. Stewart did even better in 2011. He won five of the 10 Chase races. His exciting win in the final race gave him the Sprint Cup championship for the third time.

Stewart celebrates his 2011 Sprint Cup championship after winning the Ford 400.

STEWART'S LEGACY

Stewart is one of the greatest drivers of his era. He can win on any type of track. Among active drivers, only Jimmie Johnson and Jeff Gordon had more titles through 2012. With his talent, there is no reason Stewart cannot match—or even pass—these two legends of the sport.

Stewart crosses the
finish line first at a
2012 race at Las Vegas
Motor Speedway.

TIMELINE

1971

Anthony Wayne Stewart is born on May 20 in Columbus, Indiana.

1987

Stewart wins the World Karting Association championship.

1997

Stewart wins the IRL championship.

1999

Stewart begins racing Cup Series full-time.

2002

Stewart wins his first Cup Series title.

2005

Stewart wins his second Cup Series title.

2009

Stewart becomes part owner of Stewart-Hass racing. He drives the No. 14 car.

2011

Stewart wins a tiebreaker to win his third Sprint Cup title. He becomes the first owner/ driver to win a title since 1992.

GLOSSARY

Chase
The last 10 races of the NASCAR Cup Series. Only the top 10 drivers and two wild cards qualify to race in the Chase.

Cup Series
NASCAR's top series for professional stock car drivers. It has been called the Sprint Cup Series since 2008.

grille
A metal grate at the front of a car that allows air into the radiator.

IndyCar
A type of race car with one seat and open wheels without frames around them.

open-wheel car
A race car with wheels that sit outside the car's main body.

owner
The person who owns an entire racing team. This person hires everyone on the team, including the driver and the crew.

pits
The area on a racetrack where cars can get fuel, new tires, and adjustments.

pole
The car with the fastest time in qualifying; this car starts first in a race.

rookie
A driver in his or her first full-time season in a new series.

stock car
Race cars that resemble models of cars that people drive every day.

United States Auto Club
An organization that governs several racing series for vehicles including sprint cars and midgets.

INDEX